ROUTLEDGE LII
            JL

Volume 3

ABC OF JUNG'S PSYCHOLOGY

ABC OF JUNG'S PSYCHOLOGY

JOAN CORRIE

Routledge
Taylor & Francis Group
LONDON AND NEW YORK

First published in 1927

This edition first published in 2015
by Routledge
27 Church Road, Hove BN3 2FA

and by Routledge
711 Third Avenue, New York, NY 10017

Routledge is an imprint of the Taylor & Francis Group, an informa business

© 1927 Joan Corrie

All rights reserved. No part of this book may be reprinted or reproduced or utilised in any form or by any electronic, mechanical, or other means, now known or hereafter invented, including photocopying and recording, or in any information storage or retrieval system, without permission in writing from the publishers.

Trademark notice: Product or corporate names may be trademarks or registered trademarks, and are used only for identification and explanation without intent to infringe.

British Library Cataloguing in Publication Data
A catalogue record for this book is available from the British Library

ISBN: 978-0-415-82179-7 (Set)
eISBN: 978-1-315-75425-3 (Set)
ISBN: 978-1-138-79336-1 (Volume 3)
eISBN: 978-1-315-76122-0 (Volume 3)
Pb ISBN: 978-1-138-79859-5 (Volume 3)

Publisher's Note
The publisher has gone to great lengths to ensure the quality of this reprint but points out that some imperfections in the original copies may be apparent.

Disclaimer
The publisher has made every effort to trace copyright holders and would welcome correspondence from those they have been unable to trace.

A B C
OF
JUNG'S PSYCHOLOGY

BY
JOAN CORRIE

WITH FOUR DIAGRAMS

LONDON:
KEGAN PAUL, TRENCH, TRUBNER & CO., LTD.,
BROADWAY HOUSE: 68–74, CARTER LANE, E.C.

Printed in Great Britain by
MACKAYS LTD., CHATHAM.

To
DR JUNG
AFFECTIONATELY AND GRATEFULLY

CONTENTS

PAGE

CHAPTER I
THE MIND AND ITS STRUCTURE 11

CHAPTER II
THE MIND AND ITS FUNCTIONS 27

CHAPTER III
THE MIND AND ITS DISTURBANCES ... 55

CHAPTER IV
THE SIGNIFICANCE OF DREAMS 69

NOTE

This little book is not intended to be an exposition of modern psychology. It is an attempt to place before the educated layman the principal psychological views and theories of Dr Jung of Zurich, in simple and untechnical language: his own published works being, for the most part, too scientific and abstruse for the general reader who is not a psychologist. Each statement made in its pages, therefore, is to be understood as an expression of Jung's point of view. I am responsible only for the form in which it is cast.

In England Jung is all too little known. His name is occasionally seen bracketed with that of Freud, as though their views were identical; whereas the truth is that they are largely irreconcilable. Both independent pioneers, they came into contact for a time, but their paths diverged very soon, and now very little thought in common remains. It is the

NOTE

relatively greater simplicity of Freud's psychology which has caused it to become more widely known and to enjoy a greater vogue.

For thirty years Jung has patiently pursued his investigations. He has explored the mental processes of all sorts and conditions of men—cultured and simple, European and Eastern, neurotic and the so-called normal. He has lived with Pueblo Indians and East-African primitives, and has thus acquired a knowledge of the human mind which is certainly not exceeded in our time.

Having been a pupil of Jung for some years, I have been distressed from time to time at the misunderstanding and ignorance of his work which seem to prevail. When, therefore, it was suggested to me that a short and simple outline of his principal theories might lead to a better understanding, I was glad to attempt to supply it.

It only remains to thank Dr Jung very cordially for his kindness in reading the work in manuscript.

J.C.

Zurich.
    May, 1927.

A B C OF JUNG'S PSYCHOLOGY

CHAPTER I

THE MIND AND ITS STRUCTURE

THE human psyche, or mind, is not a homogeneous whole. Part of it we are aware of as consciousness; the greater part we do not know at all, except through its effects, for we are not conscious of its operations. The apt simile of an iceberg has been used to illustrate this point. As is the top of an iceberg protruding one-tenth of its bulk above the surface of the water to the vast remainder sunk in the ocean depths, so is the conscious to the unconscious mind—relatively a very small thing.

The centre of consciousness, its focal point, is the ego; and consciousness is simply awareness of relations between its contents and the "I" who perceives them. It is *I* who am aware of the sense-perceptions, the

THE MIND

thoughts, feelings, and memories within my field of consciousness at any given moment. Without this relatedness of the 'I,' psychic processes may be active, but they are no longer conscious. The ego, however, is not the subject or self. That includes the entire psyche, both conscious and unconscious.

That part of the conscious mind which comes into relation with the external world is the personality, or *persona*[1]. It is the individual's mode of adaptation to the world, his character as it appears to be and as he often himself conceives it; but it is by no means the whole of his character, for it leaves out the unconscious elements. The *persona* is formed by environment, by training, by all the various reactions to external reality, and by the selection of such conscious psychic elements as are consonant with the man's aim in life. When the ego is identified with the *persona*; i.e. when the individual regards himself as being only what he seems to be to himself and to others, his apprehension of his own nature is extremely limited and one-sided, for he is in reality at once much

---

[1] From *personare* = to sound through: *persona* was the mask used by old-time actors.

ITS STRUCTURE

greater—and much smaller—than he imagines. We speak of certain inconsistencies of conduct as being so 'unlike' a particular person. They are only unlike his usual adaptation, or *persona*, and are perfectly consistent with his character as a whole. This identification is very frequent, and is sometimes responsible for the tragedies which occur from time to time when some honoured name is dragged in the dust in consequence of conduct running counter to the law or to morality, and which is in opposition to the individual's life-long behaviour. Had he known more of the unconscious possibilities within him, it would probably never have happened.

The unconscious part of the psyche is divided by Jung into *personal* and *collective*. The former contains everything that has been acquired during the person's life-time which has not been retained in the conscious. Everything that he has forgotten or has repressed, i.e. *intentionally* put out of mind on account of its painful or unpleasant nature, is there below the threshold. The wishes which are incongruous with his character as he conceives it, or desires it to

THE MIND

be, are in the personal unconscious, as well as whatever is unconsciously perceived, thought, or felt.

It will readily be discerned that the unconscious is thus compensatory to the conscious mind. All those elements of character which are weak or lacking in the *persona* are to be found in the unconscious attitude which balances it. Every exaggerated quality in the conscious will be compensated in the unconscious by its opposite. For instance, an aggressive, domineering person will be unconsciously mild, or even timid, on the other side : which is the reason why a man may be a tyrant to those who work under him and be hen-pecked at home. His overbearingness is the shield of his defence from the world. When the ascetic has succeeded in repressing the evil side of his nature, he may be assured that it is flourishing below the threshold—all the more dangerous because no longer faced consciously. For the truth is, that man by nature is neither black nor white, but grey ; and he who believes that the darker shades can be eliminated by the simple process of forgetting or refusing to acknowledge them

[14]

ITS STRUCTURE

is apt to be reminded by some sudden irruption from the unconscious. The threshold is relative, and the contents below are always striving to rise into consciousness.

Unconscious motives frequently prompt actions which we consciously ascribe to quite other—and generally better—motives. These give rise to those slips of speech or action which are known as psychopathological errors. An interesting example of the former is given by Dr van der Hoop of Amsterdam in his book *Character and the Unconscious*[1]. One of his patients who was not very well off said to him one day on leaving his consulting-room: 'I have no money with me to-day to pay your fee, but I will forget it next time.' A patient of the late Dr Constance Long said to her on one occasion: ' My illness is spoiling my life, and *I don't want to get well.*' There was an unconscious motive for continuing to be ill.

I have said that the mind as a whole is not homogeneous; but when we come to the collective unconscious we come to a universal

[1] Van der Hoop, *Character and the Unconscious* (International Library of Psychology), London: Kegan Paul & Co.; New York: Harcourt Brace & Co., 1923.

THE MIND

and uniform substratum common to all humanity, because it is the historical background from which every mentality has evolved. Man is the 'heir of all the ages' by virtue of the collective unconscious. It is the soil formed by age-long deposits of mental processes in which the roots of the psyche are deeply imbedded. It is 'that remnant of ancient humanity and the centuries-old past in all people, namely, the common property left behind from all development which is given to all men, like the sunshine and the rain.'[1] Every experience passed through by man in his long ascent from lower forms of life has left its mark in the psyche; for even as physically the germ-cells pass unchanged from one generation to another, so traces of experiences lived through ancestrally, and repeated millions of times, are imprinted in the structure of the brain, and, handed down through the centuries, reappear in dreams and in otherwise unaccountable reactions. The mind of the new-born babe is no mere *tabula rasa*, but contains all the potentialities

[1] Jung, *Psychology of the Unconscious*, p. 301. London: Kegan Paul & Co., Ltd., 1922.

ITS STRUCTURE

derived from his heritage human and pre-human. He brings his instincts with him, for he knows as well how to nourish himself on the first day of life as on the last.

Primeval man faced by the stupendous forces of nature against which his puny strength was useless, and surrounded by objects full of awe and mystery, apprehended his world in terms of spirit, energy, gods, demons, ghosts, dragons, etc. Such images imprinted in the brain substance evolved into sun and moon-myths, vegetation-myths, myths of gods and their death and resurrection, or of fire brought from heaven—themes found everywhere among all peoples. These imprints Jung names *primordial images* or *archetypes*. They are the forms into which repeated ancestral experiences have moulded the typically human mode of apprehension. Modern man with his scientific grasp of natural law no longer has need of myth, but the images of the past survive in his unconscious, reappear in his dreams, and constantly affect his life, because, though no effort of will can bring up any part of the collective unconscious into consciousness, its

THE MIND

contents are always striving to rise and succeeding in ways unsuspected.

Since the unconscious contains the past, it must also contain the germs of the future. All the possibilities of the individual are contained within it: some never realized, others latent until the time is ripe for their development. The inspiration of the artist, the writer, the orator, as also of the scientist himself, rises from the collective unconscious. It has forgotten nothing that has happened since Pithecanthropus (the man-ape) appeared on the earth. It is illimitable in extent. If this statement should appear to be an exaggeration, I would refer the reader to the laboratory experiments of Dr Eugene Osty of Paris and the late Dr Geley.

Further, the collective unconscious is the source from which the dynamism of psychic life proceeds. This is the *libido*. The Freudian use of this word is entirely sexual, but Jung has evolved a concept of it as psychic energy which manifests itself in as great variety of directions as life itself, and is capable of as many transformations and interchanges as is physical energy. This psychic energy or *libido* is expressed in

ITS STRUCTURE

instinct, desire, and function, and it varies in intensity, form, direction, and aim. The transformations and variations appear to have the effect of increasing and diminishing the *libido*, but it may be assumed that this is not really the case, but that the direction only has been changed. To take an example: When a person becomes depressed and listless, losing interest in his business, his pleasures, and the external affairs of life generally, it looks as if energy were lost. It is usually because the *libido* is turned within instead of without, and is concentrated upon the images and phantasies of the unconscious. It may be, and often is, that after such a period of introversion the renewed energy once more flows outwards to the external world able to accomplish what before was impossible.

The *libido* is the creative principle of life, animating all conscious purposes. Every great work of art, every achievement of science, every successful business enterprise has its inception in the *libido* of its originator.

I am indebted to Dr Jung for the two following diagrams. The first will show at a glance the evolution of the individual mind

THE MIND

from the first dawn of life up through the racial and ancestral strata. The second shows Jung's conception of the structure of the psyche.

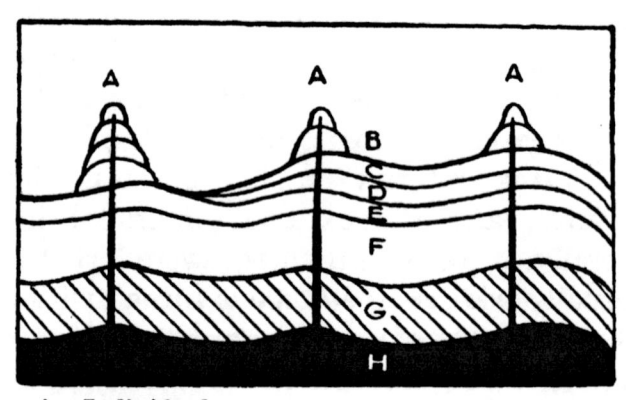

A = Individuals
B = Families
C = Clans
D = Nations
E = Large groups (European man, for example)
F = Primate Ancestors
G = Animal ancestors in general
H = Life in general

Fig. 1

About Fig. 1 nothing need be said. Who can trace the complicated influences which have evolved the first speck of protoplasm up through the millennia of years and the successive Ages of this old planet, through all the pre-human stages to produce at last

[20]

ITS STRUCTURE

man? Who can compute the struggle, the death, the seeming waste of life, and of all that goes to make it, before a nation is born,

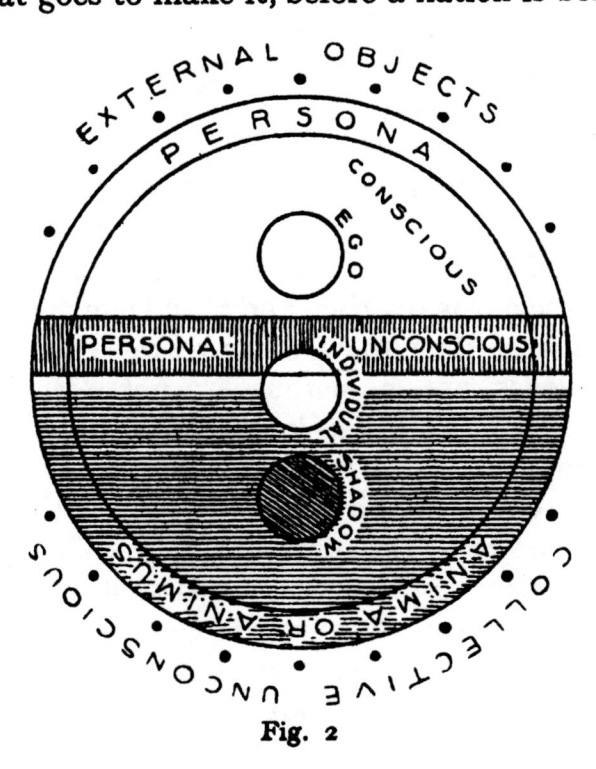

Fig. 2

before a mathematician or a poet emerges from the welter of sinew and brain?

The second diagram requires a few words to supplement it.

The psyche is here represented by a circle

[21]

THE MIND

divided into slightly uneven halves. The outer rim of the upper half shows the *persona* constantly in contact with the objects of the external world. The focus of consciousness is represented by a small circle which may be in the centre, or nearer to either the *persona* or the unconscious, according as the individual tends to identify himself with one or the other, or with neither. The threshold separating the conscious from the personal unconscious is relative, and may be higher or lower according to whether repressions and complexes are numerous or not. If the former, consciousness is contracted and the threshold is higher; if the latter, consciousness is enlarged and heightened. The threshold between the personal and collective unconscious is absolute, and volition can exercise no control over the contents below it. The slightly larger division of the circle stands for the individual's share of the racial inheritance called by Jung the ' collective unconscious.' It, like the conscious, has its focal point or centre—the shadow. It is so called because in dreams it is personified as a lesser ego, a smaller edition, as it were, or even a caricature, of the dreamer.

ITS STRUCTURE

The lower outer rim marked *anima* represents a personification of the unconscious balancing the *persona*, which Jung calls the soul (not in the Christian sense) or *anima*. True to its compensating or balancing principle, the soul or unconscious of a man is feminine, that of a woman is masculine—the *animus*. It will readily be conceded that every person is psychologically bi-sexual. In man the feminine elements, and in woman the masculine traits, are alike unconscious. The *anima* is in contact with the objects of the inner reality—the images of the collective unconscious—as the *persona* is in contact with the objects of external reality. The *anima* is an archetypal figure that might almost be described as the precipitate of man's age-long impressions of woman—not his conscious reasoned ideas, but the unconscious inherited mould into which she is cast. The *anima* appears frequently in dreams; sometimes in literature. To some men who are in close contact with their unconscious she is as real as a living woman. Sometimes the figure is projected upon a real woman, as was the case with Dante's Beatrice. Every English reader is familiar

THE MIND

with Rider Haggard's famous novel *She*, and its sequels. *She* is a typical *anima* figure, partaking of the characteristics of the images of the collective unconscious: half goddess, half dæmonic; alluring, repelling; beautiful, loving, submissive woman, and detestable, jealous murderess. *She* is the *anima*, or personification of Holly's unconscious, as Leo the hero is his *persona*.

The *animus* is not a persistent unvarying figure as is the *anima*, but a constantly changing one. The typical woman finds her conscious feeling expression centred in one person of the opposite sex: she is monogamous. But her unconscious is apparently polygamous, for the name of her *animus* might be 'legion.' He represents the *logos* principle, the masculine reason of her unconscious nature. The figure is projected in dreams on to father or husband, friend and enemy alike.

It must not be supposed that because the unconscious of a man is feminine, and the unconscious of a woman masculine, these are equal to the true or perfect masculinity and femininity. They are inferior and more or less archaic, because unconscious. When

ITS STRUCTURE

they rush up and overbalance the conscious qualities, we get the effeminate man and the '*animus*-ridden' woman. The latter does not show the logical judgment of a man: she has dogged opinions taken over ready-made from someone on to whom she has projected the *animus* figure—most likely the father, a clergyman, or favourite brother. She is like a University student of my acquaintance who told the unfortunate lecturer whose task it was to criticize her essays that he might harry her facts as much as he pleased, but she was *ready to die for her opinions!*

I have left the most important part of Fig. 2 to the last. This is the little circle in the centre marked 'Individual.' It stands for the deepest core and essence of self, that which makes a man not merely a person among other persons but a unique self among all other selves. Every human being has the germ of individuality within him, but for the most part it is unconscious. Just as we all have the same features and yet no two faces are identical, so each mind should be different from all other minds in spite of their common characteristics. We all start

THE MIND

with the ordinary collective standards of thought and conduct, and it is possible so to conform to these that differences of mentality are practically obliterated. When this happens, it means the death of individuality. Every man has the germ of something within him which makes him different from all other men; something peculiar which makes him an individual. This does not lead to isolation, for it is only by taking his place as a unit in the social whole, and by contact with other selves, that a man may differentiate himself from them, and arrive at a knowledge of his own unique selfhood which is, according to the *Upanishads*, ' smaller than the small, greater than the great.'[1]

[1] Quoted by Jung, *Psychological Types*, p. 245 (International Library of Psychology). London: Kegan Paul & Co.; New York: Harcourt Brace & Co., 1923.

CHAPTER II

THE MIND AND ITS FUNCTIONS

ACCORDING to Jung, there are four basic functions or forms of psychic activity, viz., thinking, feeling, sensation, and intuition.

The kind of thinking here referred to is not passive thought which comes and goes, but active or directed thought, controlled by the laws of logic.

Feeling is appreciation of values—not an intellectual judgment, but one which is expressed in terms of rejection or acceptance: 'I like this,' 'I dislike that.' Feeling is essentially subjective. It is *my* feeling, even though directed towards an object. Sometimes it is a mood—a 'feeling' of sadness or cheerfulness. It can be mixed with sensation, as when a beautiful or unpleasant sight or sound evokes pleasure or distaste; but in its pure form feeling is a separate function from sensation. It is not emotion, though intensity of feeling results in emotion,

THE MIND

which is always characterized by bodily disturbances. Thought and feeling are both rational functions, since feeling valuation when the function is differentiated, as well as intellectual judgment, alike proceed according to the law of reason.

Sensation and intuition are irrational functions, since both are merely perceptual. Sensation perceives what *is* in the present moment; intuition sees what may be in the future. The latter is perception of possibilities. These four functions give us four different modes of approach to the world.

We all think—or we believe we think—we all feel, and we all have sensations and intuitions. But we have them in very varying degree. In no one, it may safely be asserted, are the four functions equally developed. Owing to natural inherited disposition and to environment, every individual adapts himself to reality most easily and most successfully by means of one function, called the *superior function*. And always one lags behind relatively undeveloped and partially unconscious—the *inferior function*.

This brings us face to face with four very distinctly marked types of persons: he who

[28]

ITS FUNCTIONS

meets every situation by cool, logical thought, shaping his actions by its conclusions, and in whom feeling is relatively undeveloped; necessarily so, for feeling interrupts and interferes with logical thinking; he—or more frequently she—whose highly differentiated feeling is the instrument of valuation and adaptation, thought being relatively inferior, for the reason given above; the sensation-type, weak in intuition, but keenly quick to perceive everything given through the senses, as well as all bodily innervations; and, lastly, the intuitive-type, inferior as regards sensation, but intensely alive to all the possibilities of a situation.

The two following diagrams are taken from a set of unpublished lectures given in Zurich by Jung in 1925. The first shows the four functions in their opposition. Where thought is the superior function, feeling is the inferior one. Where intuition is the chief function, sensation is relatively weak and undeveloped.

The second diagram (Fig. 4) shows the connection of the four functions. 'Let us start with thinkng, or pure intellect. This as a rational function is connected with the irrational

THE MIND

function intuition, by what we call speculative thinking, or intuitive thinking. Then we pass to the polar opposite of thinking, namely feeling through intuitive feeling. From there to the polar opposite of intuition, sensation, *via* emotion. Emotion is that sort

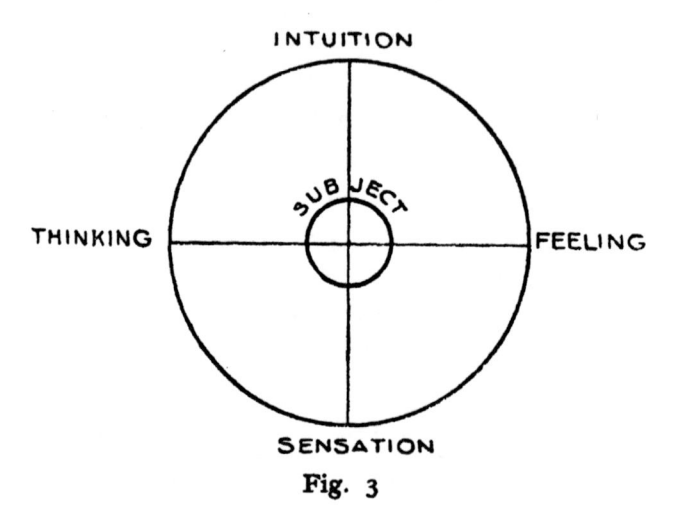

Fig. 3

of feeling which is a physiological condition, and which is perceived by sensation. From sensation we get back again to thinking through a kind of thinking we call empirical, i.e. thinking to the fact. We have now the conception that thinking passes by easy transition to both intuition or sensation,

ITS FUNCTIONS

or *vice versa*, but that it is furtherest removed from feeling.'[1]

Each of the above four function-types will

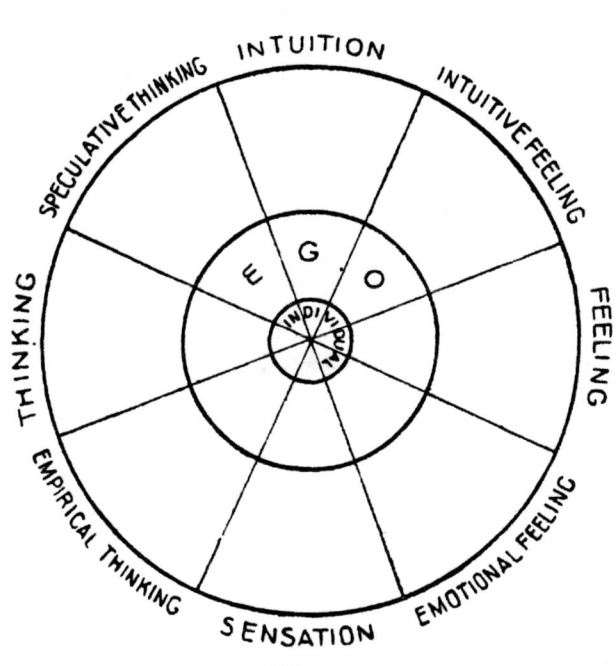

Fig. 4

come under a further category, namely that of the 'extraverted' or 'introverted' type. Observers of human nature have long pointed out sharp distinctions which have led them

[1] Jung, *Lectures* (unpublished).

THE MIND

to classify men according to their temperamental differences; as, for example, James has described in his *Varieties of Religious Experience*'[1] the 'tough-minded' and the 'tender-minded' man; but Jung has worked out in fine detail from his long experience two fundamentally opposite types which he calls general-attitude types, and to which he has severally given the names of 'extravert' and 'introvert.' They are distinguished by the attitude adopted in each case towards the object. The *libido*, or psychic energy, or interest, of the extravert flows outwards to the object: objective facts or external happenings are the all-important factors of life for him. People and things and events are endlessly interesting to him, and he adapts himself easily and well to his environment. He is the man with 'many irons in the fire,' and is never so happy as when his days are full to overflowing with business or other activities. He talks fluently, makes friends readily, and is in general a useful and appreciated member of society. His nature is extensive but not intensive, and whatever

[1] W. James, *Varieties of Religious Experience*. London and New York: Longmans & Co., 1902.

ITS FUNCTIONS

else he knows he never knows his own soul. He is eminently social and detests solitude. Any sort of self-knowledge he usually characterizes as morbid, and his moral and social values are those of his environment and time.

The attitude of the introvert is diametrically opposite. His interest is fundamentally subjective and not objective, and, for this reason, he is often considered by the undiscriminating to be more selfish than the extravert, whose sympathies *apparently* flow out to one and all. This judgment is, however, entirely superficial. Neither introvert nor extravert has any monopoly of selfishness. For the introvert the significance of the object lies not in itself but in how it appears to him. It is not the situation objectively considered, but the situation *as he sees it*, that is the decisive factor. The first reaction of the introvert to the object is apt to be a negative one. Whereas the extravert, so to speak, enfolds the world in his arms, and cheerfully seeks adventure therein, full of faith in its benevolence towards himself, the introvert is never quite at home in the external world of men and things. He views it with more or less sus-

THE MIND

picion and fear, and unable to adapt easily to it, withdraws into himself, into his own inner kingdom, where he is quite at home. He can not only endure solitude, which would break the extravert : a certain amount of it is necessary to his mental health and happiness. As a rule, self-expression is difficult to him, and he is apt to appear dull and uninteresting. Those who thus judge are little aware of the multitudinous activity going on within. Because of the lack of expression, introverts are frequently misunderstood. Introverts and extraverts can never really understand each other, for their differences are polar ; yet, perhaps because of that fact, they have a strange attraction for each other. This is often seen in the choice of husband or wife. Because each type is complementary to the other such marriages are successful up to a point, the outgoing tendency of the one partner balancing the introverting attitude of the other in all matters of external welfare, but the soul union which is the essence of true marriage can rarely be attained between a typical extravert and a typical introvert for lack of complete mutual comprehension.

ITS FUNCTIONS

While all this is absolutely true, it is no less true that every human being extraverts, and every human being introverts. The two attitudes are like the swing of a pendulum in first one direction, and then the opposite one. It is the *conscious* attitude which has been described above, and according as its preponderating habit is to flow out to the object or to withdraw from the object, do we get the type.

The unconscious of the extravert is introverted; that of the introvert is extraverted. Both are inferior to the conscious attitude of the opposite type. Because the introvert consciously withdraws from the object asserting the superiority of his ego, unconsciously the object dominates him and fills him with fear. For example, an introvert always wants to preserve his freedom of action. He hates to feel bound by circumstances to adopt a certain course. He will not take the objective factors of his life sufficiently into consideration. Because he struggles to maintain his subjective freedom against the just claims of the object, unconsciously he is apt to become riveted, as it were, by unbreakable fetters to some objective situation which

[35]

THE MIND

assumes alarming proportions, and may even fill him with panic. He gets into a 'hole' and cannot get out. The extravert would climb out with ease—or, rather, he would never get in—because he would give the objective situation its proper value from the beginning. The collective unconscious of the introvert is outside him in the external world. That is to say, his racial memories, his primordial images or archetypes, are reanimated by situations which occur in his ordinary objective life. These images rising up from the mists of long-past centuries and unconsciously applied to the difficult situation of the moment fill him with dread.

In the case of the extravert, whose conscious life is spent amid objects and external events, it is his unconscious subjective life he views with suspicion and fear. He has a great resistance to introspection, and prefers to know nothing about that side of himself. But an ostrich-like policy is never successful. His personal unconscious is full of repressed subjective tendencies, which from lack of expression are infantile in character. His ego, denied suitable conscious value in view of the overpowering influence exercised over him

ITS FUNCTIONS

by the object, may burst forth as unconscious egotism, or some 'nervous' illness may thwart his too-extraverted activities. The archetypal images of the collective unconscious are reanimated by his own unconscious tendencies—not by the situations of external life as in the case of the introvert—and autonomous units or ancestral modes of thought or behaviour may rise, which will completely change the man's character and ruin the carefully built structure of his life. For any one-sided mode of living will inevitably give rise to reprisals from the unconscious. Jung gives several instances in *Psychological Types* of how the unconscious can interfere when extraversion passes reasonable limits. It will depend on the function-type to which the man belongs whether he is betrayed by his thinking, his feelings, his sensations, or his intuitions.

Each function, as we have said, can be either extraverted or introverted. In the beginning Jung identified thought with the introvert and feeling with the extravert, but later experience showed him there were 'introverts who do not think, and extraverts who do not feel.'

THE MIND

The thinking of the extravert is of the empirical or sometimes the intuitive kind. He orders his life in accordance with logical conclusions, arrived at through consideration of facts of objective experience or of generally accepted principles. He accumulates facts, for which he has the greatest possible respect; his thought is impersonal and constructive He readily finds a rôle to fit him as natural scientist, politician, financier, advocate, ecclesiastic, architect, engineer, or any line where constructive ability of an objective kind is required. Owing to the inflexibility of his intellectual judgments, when the type is extreme he is apt to be intolerant, fanatical, even tyrannical; as, for example, a Torquemada; or, on a smaller scale, the domestic tyrant. Feeling is rigidly repressed; hence there is scant sympathy for others unless they conform to his views of life. Mere irrational perceptions are permitted no place in his scheme of things; but, as life is never regulated by logic alone, these find a place in the unconscious. Here the one-sidedness of the conscious attitude is compensated by personal sensitiveness, infantile feelings, doubts, and irrational superstitions.

ITS FUNCTIONS

When thought is the superior function of the introvert, it is subjective, i.e., it is not concerned with the intrinsic nature of the object but with the subject's own special idea of it, which idea has birth within himself. It is the idea, not the fact, which counts. The ideas of the extravert rise out of the objective fact, and he will seek confirmation through yet more facts. The ideas of the introvert rise from the primordial images within himself.

Perhaps it may be well to remind the reader once more of the nature of a primordial image, or archetype, to which reference has been made in Chapter I. It is an inherited predisposition of the mind to view a situation according to the unconscious impression left by millions of similiar situations experienced ancestrally. We have made our brains during the process of ascent, and they are as they are because our ancestors have behaved in certain ways when placed in the various situations of life. They have loved, fought dragons, been entrapped, faced the dangerous ghosts of the lonely forests, and so on. We, their descendants, no longer fight actual dragons or fear the supernatural. But, for

THE MIND

all that, we find ourselves constantly in situations which could be metaphorically described as above, and then the images, the archetypes, stamped indelibly in the brain substance become re-animated, and we see ' with the mind's eye ' an archaic picture of the conscious situation as viewed by the unconscious.

Such images welling up from the unconscious are the germ of the subjective ideas of the thinking introvert, and he seeks to fit the objective facts to them. If these will not altogether fit, he may even force them into the ideal mould. His thought is not merely constructive like that of the extravert. It is theoretical, creative, and sometimes mystical. ' Facts are collected as evidence or examples of a theory, but never for their own sake.'[1] Like all introverts, he shows his worst side to the world. Feeling being repressed, he appears cold and inconsiderate. He is dogmatic and unyielding with respect to his ideas, tenacious of their validity, and tactless in the manner of their presentation. Misunderstood or even disliked by those who know him least, and whom he keeps at arm's

[1] Jung, *Psychological Types*, p. 481.

ITS FUNCTIONS

length, he is most appreciated by those who are nearest to him and who know him best.

We now come to the extraverted and introverted feeling-types. Like thought, feeling is a rational function expressing a judgment, in this case of values.

Feeling is an essentially feminine characteristic, and as a differentiated function of adaptation it is less frequently found in men, whose superior function is more often thought.

The extraverted feeling-type is objective. That is, the kind of feeling induced depends entirely upon the object itself, or upon generally accepted standards of valuation. He accepts or rejects, likes or dislikes that which is commonly accepted or rejected; and finds good, true, and beautiful what the judgment of his time and generation finds good and true and beautiful. Feeling being differentiated—i.e., specialized—is under control, and he is able so to direct it as to feel what he 'ought' to feel in any given objective situation. Up to a point, this makes for harmony with the environment and good-feeling. The feeling-extravert extends a

THE MIND

warm easy sense of fellowship and sociability around when kindly disposed, which is very pleasant. When the type is at all extreme, the feeling shown tends to become affected and insincere. In any case, it is extensive and not intensive, for the feeling-extravert does not feel. This seems a paradox; but if feeling be so centred in the object as to constitute virtual at-one-ness with it, then none can be left over for the individual's own experience. Thought is relatively repressed, otherwise it would interfere with the feeling values. No one whose thinking is permitted full effect can always feel as he 'ought' to feel in every situation; therefore the feeling-extravert turns thinking overboard when it threatens his feeling valuations. It is relegated to the unconscious, where it takes on an infantile character, and being under no control, frequently irrupts into consciousness under the guise of disturbing ideas and doubts respecting the objects—human and otherwise—upon which feeling has already passed its judgment.

The introverted feeling-type is just the opposite of the foregoing description. If one might be allowed such a metaphor, it

ITS FUNCTIONS

might be said that extraverted feeling is like a wide but shallow lake over whose smooth surface the sunlight plays or which the wind lashes into sudden fury, to be followed quickly again by gentle ripples; while introverted feeling resembles a solitary mountain-tarn, silent, dark, mysterious, whose depth no man knows. Such feeling is profound and intense. The individual feels all the time, but, as he cannot express it, he is frequently regarded as cold and lacking in feeling. He is rarely emotional outwardly, but may be torn by emotion within. His feeling is subjective, critical, and often apparently depreciative of the object, since it does not depend primarily on the object itself but on the individual's own valuation of it, which is frequently negative. His extreme sensitiveness causes him to withdraw from the object which has power to hurt, and he seems aloof though in reality he may not be so. Such a type, unable to express what he feels by reason of his lack of relatedness to objects and only succeeding in being clumsy if he attempts it, is bound to be misunderstood; which misunderstanding in turn drives him more into himself, until he

THE MIND

may become as egocentric as he is usually—but not always with justice—considered to be. Thinking being unconscious and relatively undeveloped exalts the consciously depreciated objects, so that, while consciously asserting the superiority of the subject and its feeling judgment, unconsciously his thought confers a dominating influence upon the very objects he rejects, and the external situations he encounters day by day become difficult to manage or even embittering.

The next two functions to be considered are irrational. That is, sensation and intuition are not functions of judgment but of perception. The individuals in whom one or the other is the superior function do not order their lives by logical conclusions, whether of thought or of feeling. Their perception of the accidental happenings of life is their guide-post to show them the way to go.

The extraverted sensation-type, like all other extraverts, is objective. Actual concrete objects constitute reality for him, and the amount of sensation he derives from them sums up the value of living. Sensation is,

ITS FUNCTIONS

of course, a basic function. The external world comes to everyone through sense-perception, but in the type under consideration it is perception raised to its highest level. He knows no other reality but that which causes sensation and which comes to him from without. He neither thinks nor feels much consciously—he only senses. The maximum of sensation to be got out of the object is his aim in life. He is not necessarily gross. His pleasures may be refined, and he may be a lover of beauty. But, whether sensual or refined, the strongest sensation is the greatest good, and the value of the object consists in its ability to provide this. The other functions, especially intuition, are repressed, and in the unconscious take their revenge, as is always the case when the attitude is one-sided. His poor and infantile intuition causes him to attribute to others tendencies and qualities which are really within himself. The sense of reality when pushed to an extreme in the conscious is compensated in the unconscious by ideas, imaginations, and feelings which are wholly unreal.

The introverted sensation-type stands in

THE MIND

marked contrast to that of the extravert. At first sight the name seems almost a contradiction in terms, since sense-perception must come from without. There is the object, and from it must be derived the stimulus which results in sight or sound. But it must not be forgotten that an object requires a perceiving subject in order to exist. It is *I* who perceive, and, if every perceiving subject were swept off the earth, then there would be no external world at all, *as we know it*, to be sensed. The difference between the extraverted and the introverted form of this type lies in this, that the former senses the object directly, giving himself up to its influence, while the latter rather stands off from it, and interposes his own subjective perception, his own view of it, between himself and it, thus altering its character. It is, of course, well understood that no two people ever see the external world exactly alike. But the introvert, in whom sensation predominates, perceives more in the object than is actually in it. He puts into it something which does not actually belong to it but which comes from his perception of it. Therefore the effect it produces on him is largely

ITS FUNCTIONS

his own. It cannot be gauged by the stimulus which the object is apparently calculated to supply. All sense-impressions, whether coming from the body or from the external world, are acutely perceived, and are often of an unpleasant nature. Moreover, it must not be forgotten that there are 'objects' in the unconscious upon which subjective perception readily seizes. The primordial images influence his judgment of men and things, making him behave as though the object had some magical power which of course does not belong to it. His intuition is repressed, and in a sense perverted, since, when possibilities do present themselves to him, they seem dangerous or threatening in nature. Such a type appears quiet, calm, even self-possessed, but within loom all sorts of fears and fancies, due to the over-subjectivity of perception which makes the object not as it is in reality but as it appears to him.

The intuitive-types approach the world from a totally different angle from that of sensation. Whereas the latter perceives concrete reality as it exists now at the present moment, the former sees not what *is*, but

THE MIND

what *may be*, the possibilities of the future. Sensation is like a horse with blinkers. It sees the road immediately under its nose but nothing of that which is round the corner. Intuition cannot see the road under its nose, because it is looking round the corner all the time. The two types live in different worlds. The solid facts of the sensation-type are uninteresting, even boring, to the intuitive; and the possibilities which are so full of life and promise to the latter are as bubbles filled with air to the former. Little chance there is of a mutual understanding.

The extraverted intuitive-type is always on the look-out for possibilities in the external situation; his perception is not subjective. Anything new fascinates him. New ideas, new situations, new people—all offer the new possibilities which this type craves, and, indeed, cannot exist without. His mind is constantly perceiving new combinations and alterations of existing reality in accordance with the possibilities he sees ahead. In his business or profession new vistas are constantly opening out before him. When the type is a woman, she is alive to all social opportunities and possible advantages.

ITS FUNCTIONS

These perceptions are of the utmost value for life, but that which is already existing is also of value, and the tragedy of the extraverted intuitive lies in the fact that he discards the present value for the future possibility. If one is always leaving the good which is for the good which may be, one may sometimes find it is the shadow which has been grasped and not the substance, as in the well-known fable. Sensation, being the opposite of intuition, is weak and unconscious in this type. Thought and feeling are never allowed to interfere with possibilities. The extraverted intuitive type is apt to show little consideration for other people, not because he is unkind but because he does not see their need of the moment. The unconscious asserts itself by giving rise to inferior ideas and feelings, and by compulsory ties of some sort to people, or places, or things, thus balancing in a childish way the restlessness of the conscious.

The introverted intuitive is not concerned with external facts. His perception is subjective and focussed upon the images he finds in the unconscious. His sight is turned within, and there amid the wealth of arche-

THE MIND

types he finds the material necessary for his vision. To those around him he seems to have his head in the air and no solid ground beneath his feet. To himself the images have as great an objective reality as those of the external world to the extravert. Indeed, in some cases they may even become externalized and take on a visible form. If the type is an artist, his work will be of a fantastic nature, strange and unpleasing to a rational type. Anyone who has seen the Wiertz pictures in Brussels will recall the prodigality of fantastic imagery used to express the painter's vision. Or the images may take a commanding tone and relate themselves to future events, as in the case of an Isaiah or a Jeremiah. These seemed to have their heads in the air to their contemporaries. For the introverted intuitive sensation is almost abolished. Jung tells of a patient he once had of this type who when he asked her half-jokingly if she had never noticed that she had a body, replied with all seriousness that she had not! 'She had ceased even to hear her steps when she walked—she was just floating through the world.' Naturally this is an extreme instance.

ITS FUNCTIONS

The question may perhaps be asked: Cannot introverts and extraverts deliberately try to alter the innate tendencies which when extreme prove to be disabilities? The answer must be that the type remains the same, for it is fundamental, even biological, ' due to some unconscious instinctive cause . . . Nature knows two fundamentally different ways of adaptation which determine the further existence of the living organism; the one is by increased fertility, accompanied by a relatively small degree of defensive power and individual conservation; the other is by individual equipment of manifold means of self-protection, coupled with a relatively insignificant fertility. This biological contrast seems not merely to be the analogue, but also the general foundation of our two psychological modes of adaptation. On the one hand, I need only point to the peculiarity of the extravert, which constantly urges him to spend and propagate himself in every way, and, on the other, to the tendency of the introvert to defend himself against external claims, to conserve himself from any expenditure of energy directly related to the object, thus

THE MIND

consolidating for himself the most secure and impregnable position.'[1] Occasionally as a result of early training a falsification of type may take place, the child being twisted against its nature into the opposite type, but the penalty paid is almost certain to be a neurosis in later life.

When, however, the type is extreme much can be done in suitable cases to reach individuation (a better balance of all four functions) by the method of psychological analysis. By revealing his unconscious tendencies to the extravert it teaches him to introvert and find values within himself, and by the same means the introvert learns to adapt himself with greater ease and better result to the outside world. Each needs to be guided in a different direction—the introvert without and the extravert within himself. But no person is qualified to attempt the difficult and delicate task of analysing another person's mind until his own has undergone a searching analysis at the hands of an expert.

It must be thoroughly understood that in the very slender outline of the characteristics

[1] Jung, *Psychological Types*, p. 414.

ITS FUNCTIONS

of the various types given above it is the *pure* type that has been described. In concrete cases there are individual traits which modify these characteristics, which latter also exists in varying degree. It is necessary to emphasize this, as an idea seems to obtain in some quarters that introverts and extraverts are alike morbid specimens of the race. It is not so. They are the ordinary humanity we talk with, do business with, live with all our lives, and in one or other of which categories we must place ourselves.

The reader who wishes to go deeper into the subject must be referred to Jung's *Psychological Types*, translated by Dr H. G. Baynes.

CHAPTER III

THE MIND AND ITS DISTURBANCES

MANY disturbances of the mind can be considered as issuing from unequal development of the four functions which are our means of adaptation to the world. If each were equally differentiated, or separated out from the others, to do its own special work, such disturbances would be much rarer. They are caused by the over-development of the superior function to the detriment of the others, which, deprived of their full conscious value, become more and more unconscious as *libido* is taken from them to add to the already over-weighted superior function. Only a certain amount, however, can be abstracted: for every function, every instinct has its own energy attached to it. If not suppressed to too great an extent, the unconscious tendencies act as compensatory or balancing agents to the conscious differentiated function, thus preventing too much

THE MIND

one-sidedness. But when the neglect is too great, they sink to a low level of the unconscious, to a primitive condition of culture, and in this state they act in opposition to the conscious and become destructive in character. For *libido* is always dynamic. It must create or destroy. What results is a '*conflict*,' sometimes conscious but also often unconscious. The house of psychic life is divided against itself, and conscious and unconscious may assume the attitude of civil war.

A conflict arises when a person finds himself up against a problem which cannot be solved by the superior function, and which the inferior function is inadequate to deal with. For instance, a feeling-type or a sensation-type might find himself confronted by a sudden financial crisis which only carefully directed thinking or intuition could bring to a successful issue; or a thought-type might find himself entangled in a situation from which only differentiated feeling could free him. Or the conflict can be unconscious, as in the case of a patient of Jung, an artist. He had been commissioned to paint a fresco for a church, and the subject he chose was the miracle of Pentecost. The

ITS DISTURBANCES

grouping of the apostles presented no difficulty, but when he came to the central figure, to the *miracle*, he found he could not represent it. There was an inhibition. He rejected the fire-symbol and could not replace it by another, for he did not know what the Holy Ghost was. The unconscious reacted; he had neurotic symptoms and analysis revealed that there was an unconscious conflict between conventional religion and his own conceptions. His unconscious idea of the Holy Ghost proved to be a dæmoniacal figure. Torn between these two opposing forces, he fell into a neurosis. When an obstacle occurs in life which the *libido* cannot overcome, it is heaped up in the unconscious and thus causes tension between the *pairs of opposites*.

The *libido* being the creative principle is always in movement between opposites. Everything in nature and in life has its opposite. Were it not so, knowledge as we apprehend it would cease to be, and life would become the existence of monads. We only know life through death, love through hate, good through evil, and beauty through experience of ugliness. Every high must

THE MIND

have a low, and every first a last. Every affirmative brings its own negation with it. ' So, when you say Yes, you say at the same time No. This principle may seem a hard one, but as a matter of fact there must be this split in the *libido* or nothing works and we remain inert . . . The *libido* is not split in itself: it is a case of balancing movement between opposites, and you could say that *libido* is one or that *libido* is two according as you concentrate now on the flow and now on the opposing poles between which the flow takes place. The opposition is a necessary condition of *libido* flow.'[1]

The principle of the pairs of opposites is world-wide. Very early philosophies, such as the Chinese and the Brahmanic, are based upon it. Both Lau Tse and Confucius, and later the Greek philosopher Heraclitus, teach that in time everything generates its opposite. Modern psychology—that of Freud and Adler as well as Jung's—recognizes the principle of opposition in psychic tendencies.

If this be so, and Yes and No are inherent in our mental constitution, it is readily com-

[1] Jung, *Lectures* (unpublished).

ITS DISTURBANCES

prehensible that if the affirmative be exaggerated, the negative at once rises to contradict it, and thence comes the conflict. An individual may be torn asunder between two apparently conflicting duties. Feeling, perhaps, weighs down the scale on one side, while thought insists on the greater importance of the opposite duty. Or religious agnosticism in the conscious brought about by a too intellectual reaction from rigid creeds and formulæ has to do battle with unconscious feeling which clings to the beliefs inculcated at the mother's knee. I remember the case of a young Scotsman brought up in the most rigid Calvinism. Consciously he professed to believe in nothing but 'matter' and 'force.' Unconsciously he was filled with fear and uncertainty.

When the difficulty proves insurmountable, *regression* takes place. The *libido*, unable to go forward, goes back. It sinks into the unconscious, and an earlier, more childish mode of dealing with an analogous situation takes the place of the normally adapted adult function. This is to become *neurotic*.

It must be well understood that neurosis is not the special prerogative of weak-willed,

THE MIND

feeble-minded individuals, who from birth seem destined to pursue a half-hearted and stumbling way through life. It is to be found among all classes of the community: among the most highly gifted, sensitive and intellectual, equally with hard-working peasants and artisans. Anyone, the most normal and matter-of-fact, may start a neurosis under a strain which is too great for him to support. It is a question of the limit to which he can go. True, there is often a greater sensitiveness of psychic constitution in some individuals which makes adaptation more difficult, and the breaking-point more easily reached; for neurosis is neither more nor less than inferior adaptation, 'an act of adaptation that has failed,'[1] but such may occur to either prince or ploughman.

Regression is the starting-point of all kind of symptoms, physical as well as mental, for, strange as it may seem, neurosis is an attempt to find a way out. The Great War made us familiar with serious physical symptoms, such as blindness, deafness, dumbness,

[1] Jung, *Analytical Psychology*, p. 234. London: Baillière; New York: Dodd, Mead & Co.

ITS DISTURBANCES

paralysis, for which no organic cause existed but which were psychic in origin. It depends largely on the type to which the individual belongs whether his neurotic symptoms are physical or mental. The extravert is most prone to hysteria, by which is meant bodily illness due to mental causes. The day is almost at an end when hysteria is stigmatized as 'imagination.' The term includes all functional diseases, for irregularity of function arises from neurosis, when there is no organic lesion behind it. Let an extravert lose his fortune, or have an unsuccessful love-affair, and a whole train of hysteric symptoms may arise. Indigestion—for he cannot digest life, as it is presenting itself to him—insomnia, migraine, palpitation may all afflict him. Such symptoms may also be an unconsciously engineered attempt to bring his too-extraverted mode of living to a standstill.

The neurotic symptoms of the introvert present a different picture. Here the battle is waged between the ego and the object—human or otherwise—which consciously, as has already been said, he disparages by his indifference and unrelatedness to it. Uncon-

THE MIND

sciously, according to the law of the opposites, it assumes a disproportionate importance, which threatens the superiority of his ego, to guard which is the introvert's supreme care. He is apt to identify this with the subject or self, of which it is only the conscious focal point. This leads to desire for power over the object, which nevertheless continues to dominate him. An introvert of my acquaintance who was somewhat neurotic described the effect of objects upon her as being like a too sharp impression made by a seal on wax, under which she writhed until the impression began to fade and she could forget it. Out of such desire for power, on the one hand, and domination on the other, a conflict ensues of which the individual may know nothing but its effects. He becomes a prey to emotions within. Anxiety, depression, an extreme sensitiveness both of mind and body, and always fears, beset him. If an introvert be at all neurotic, he may be said to be haunted by fear, which is in great contrast to his calm and unperturbed appearance. He may become irritable and hypochondriacal. The outcome is exhaustion, both mental and physical. Such a neurotic is tired always, and incapable of prolonged work or any other strain while the neurosis lasts. There is too great a drain of energy going on within.

Regression—a sinking back to a more or less childish level, and so seeking to escape difficulties with which one finds oneself incompetent to deal—is one way of trying to evade life. Another way is to endeavour to forget all about them.

Repression is intentional forgetting: a deliberate putting out of the mind of whatever is painful. This way denies that there is any conflict by ignoring it. It is a short-sighted policy, for the painful conscious contents thus repressed into the unconscious combine themselves into complexes, and these being under no control may work havoc with the person's life. Strictly speaking, a complex, which is a group of ideas held together by an emotional tone, can as well be conscious as unconscious. One can have a golf-complex, or a church-complex, or any other group of ideas. Such a complex would be called by academic psychology an apperception-mass. But the complexes under consideration are groups split off from consciousness which have sunk below the threshold, carrying a large portion of *libido* with them. They are independent of each other—little autonomous free lances, pathological units.

Such complexes are the cause of obsessions, compulsions, and phobias. A guilt-complex, for instance, formed by repression of some act or acts of which the person is ashamed and of which the memory is too painful to be retained in consciousness, may result in endless hand-washings or other attempts at scrupulosity of cleanliness. (Lady Macbeth's cry : ' Out, out, damned spot ! ' though a trite illustration, will at once come to mind.) Or an erotic fantasy-system rigidly repressed may produce obsessional ideas of a tormenting nature. The fear of fire, or of falling from a height, experienced by many people may be traced to similar complexes. Sometimes the obsession is compulsory in nature. The individual must touch certain objects, or avoid certain places such as open spaces or public buildings where crowds are assembled. He can always give some apparently good reason for his conduct, but

ITS DISTURBANCES

the real cause lies in some hidden autonomous complex of which he knows nothing.

An inferiority-complex, which is very frequent, may produce in the individual such a conscious impression of his own greatness as to amount to megalomania. Short of this, the conscious personality will exhibit unpleasant traits of self-assertion and superiority. Such a complex arises when a sensitive person has been consistently depreciated by those about him. An example is seen in the case of a small boy, the son of a Spanish father and a British mother. Despite the fact that he was being continually punished at school for disobedience, he always praised and justified himself. He could never—or hardly ever—be made to admit that he was wrong. Instead, he insisted that he was a very fine fellow. A kind young aunt, expostulating with him on one occasion, pointed out that it was not a British trait to be constantly ' blowing his own trumpet.' The child's answer gave the key to the situation: 'If I don't praise myself, no one else ever does.' He was being ruined by depreciation, and the feelings thus aroused had been repressed, resulting in the

THE MIND

formation of an inferiority-complex which showed itself in an apparently conceited personality.

Another symptom of unconscious complexes is *projection*. This means a throwing across of something which belongs to the subject into the object. This unconscious content is perceived in the object as though it belonged to it. For instance, a person with an inferiority-complex will project inferiority on to other people to whom consciously he feels himself superior. Possibly in some respects they are inferior, but most of it comes from his own complex. Or a person with a religious complex may project his own unconscious scepticism on to anyone whose creed seems less orthodox than his own. Again, it may happen—and frequently does—that a man may project the image of his mother into his wife, or a woman the image of her father into her husband. No words can be too strong to estimate the influence of parents upon their children. Wise and understanding parents deliberately diminish and gradually withdraw their influence as the child reaches puberty, thus teaching him to stand on his own feet, and

ITS DISTURBANCES

allowing him to learn how to live by the mistakes he makes; but the love of too many is possessive, wanting to guide and direct long after childhood is past. Where this is the case and the emotional tie is too strong, the child is bound to the parents by a kind of psychical umbilical cord, it may be for life, so that to become an individual—in the psychological sense—is impossible for him. Such a man when choosing a wife is unconsciously looking for a mother. She must be the kind of woman his mother was. We all have father and mother-complexes, and their images are part of the contents of the unconscious; but we do not all project them. It is when the child has become identified with the parent—thinking and acting as the latter thinks and acts, and not for himself as a separate and distinct personality—that projection takes place; usually with more or less disastrous consequences.

The *anima* (or *animus*) is also very frequently projected upon a real person. This takes place when the individual is unaware of his own unconscious tendencies and identifies himself with his *persona* or character as it appears to be outwardly. Then the

THE MIND

unknown part of himself is projected on to a person whose qualities are similar to his own unconscious ones. The result is to produce dependence on that person, and an emotional tie of an overwhelming and compulsory nature. There can be no indifference to the carrier of the projection. Such a person is bound to be either loved or hated.

Seeing that the unconscious can so interfere with our lives, it would appear to be the part of wisdom to endeavour to learn somewhat of our own hidden tendencies. How this can best be accomplished will be discussed in the following chapter.

CHAPTER IV

The Significance of Dreams

The significance of dreams lies in the fact that they provide an incomparable way of becoming acquainted with the contents of the unconscious mind. They are psychic processes which are active during sleep, the period of conscious inactivity but of the maximum of unconscious energy; from which it seems reasonable to conclude that dreams offer the royal road to a better understanding of what goes on in us below the threshold.

By day the unconscious irrupts into the conscious life, causing speech and action of which we are either unaware, or, because we do not recognize it as consistent with our character, we like to say we did not intend; but at night the unconscious has the field to itself, and the dream depicts that side. The picture it presents balances the conscious point of view by exhibiting an aspect of one-

THE MIND

self or of the situation which it has not taken into account, sometimes in a sardonic way, as in the following example. A gentleman who was undergoing psychological analysis dreamed that he and his doctor went fishing, and that they caught an *octopus*. The chief impression given by this man was one of overvaluation of himself. His conceit appeared boundless, and, as a matter of fact, he was a megalomaniac. The dream contained a warning on the part of the unconscious that this overestimation of his powers constituted a danger in the depths of his nature which, if not recognized for what it was, would destroy him. It was a picture of his psychological state at that time.

There are still people who maintain that dreams arise from physical causes such as indigestion, a noise, a light, etc.; but they never explain why the imagery of the dream should be so pertinent. Why did not the fishermen in the foregoing dream catch a whale or a shark? Because neither would so fitly represent the destructive action of overweening conceit as an octopus: the paralysing effect of the deadly tentacles on

SIGNIFICANCE OF DREAMS

first one function and then another, and the slow dragging-down from the light and air of reality into the depths of the unconscious, where adaptation to life is impossible.

The unconscious being more primitive than the conscious, its language is primitive also. It is symbolic and allegorical, expressing itself by images. It says: 'It is as if things were like this.' As is well known, Freud regards the dream as the expression of a wish that has been repressed because it is incompatible with the dreamer's conscious ideals. Jung's view is much wider. He looks upon the dream as 'the subliminal picture of the psychological condition of the individual in his waking state'—that is, it gives the other side which is unknown in the waking state. ' In the conscious process of reflection it is indispensable that, so far as possible, we should realize all the aspects and consequences of a problem, in order to find the right solution. This process is continued automatically in the more or less unconscious state of sleep, where . . . all those other points of view occur to the dreamer (at least by way of allusion) that during the day were under-estimated or even

THE MIND

totally ignored; in other words, were comparatively unconscious.'[1]

Behind the manifest content of the dream as it is remembered is always a latent or hidden content, and to understand it associative material is required. The free associations of the dreamer (whatever comes into his mind when considering the dream, however apparently irrelevant) bring up thoughts, feelings, and memories which are entirely pertinent and necessary to the understanding of the dream. To get at the full meaning of any dream it must be dissected into its constituent parts, and each fragment examined in the light of the given associations.

Dreams can be regarded either objectively or subjectively. When the figures introduced are *real persons*, and the origin of the dream comes from incidents, trains of thought, or impressions connected with the immediate past mixed with memories of the earlier life, then it can be taken objectively, because each associated memory is related to actual conditions. Such a dream comes

[1] *Analytical Psychology*, p. 222.

SIGNIFICANCE OF DREAMS

from the personal unconscious, and the lower levels, those of the collective unconscious, are untouched.

But when the dream-symbols are not real objects but images from the collective unconscious, then 'the whole dream is the dreamer' (Jung). That is to say, the different parts of the dream, instead of being referred to existing conditions, are ascribed to the dreamer himself. Each detail is taken as representing a quality or tendency in the psychology of the subject who dreams, his free associations pointing to the meaning. This is interpretation on the subjective plane.

When the analysis of a dream leads back to the earlier life and finds the cause for the dreamer's present situation in some event or set of circumstances in the past, then it is reductive and the interpretation is causal. The Freudian method of dream-analysis is always causal-reductive.

It is not so with Jung. His mode of dream interpretation is not merely reductive and objective: he considers them on the subjective plane as well. It is prospective as well as retrospective. He does not

THE MIND

believe that the only factors which explain an individual are either his past life, or even his ancestry. There are tendencies in the mental life of the present which will lead to future possibilities of development, and these must be taken into account. There is a meeting-point in every dream of past, present, and future and the synthesis points to the way to take.

'Dreams being the expression of the moment must be both of the past and also leading toward a future, and therefore they cannot be understood by the causal principle alone. We can understand a process that shows developmental movement only by taking it both as a product of the past and as an originator of something to come. I hold that psychology cannot identify with causality alone, but that we need another view-point as well. The system we deal with is self-regulating and so the principle of purposiveness is included in it. Particularly does the nervous system show purposive reflexes, and for that reason, anything born out of the psyche has a purposive side. . . . You can push causes back indefinitely, but it is only procrastination

SIGNIFICANCE OF DREAMS

when you do; for what matters is the present moment.'[1]

In a fairly recent book the author, speaking of psycho-analysis, says: 'Nothing is done, positively, to bring the mind nearer to the fulness of its own nature. The work is negative.'

'Psycho-analysis' is a Freudian term, and, strictly speaking, should be limited to the reductive method employed by Freud and his followers. Jung calls his procedure 'analytical psychology.' This is not a mere matter of words; for Freud objects to the term he invented being used by other schools, and as we have seen, Jung's mode of analysing is totally different.

But the book alluded to was not speaking of Freud, but of modern psychology in general. The above quotation shows the misunderstanding abroad respecting Jung and his work. If the purposeful quality of a dream is taken into consideration, it points the way to the realization of greater fulness of the dreamer's nature, which is indeed the goal aimed at in analytical psychology.

[1] Jung, *Lectures* (unpublished).

THE MIND

There can be no fulness of the mind's nature without some knowledge of its deeper layers. 'We have analysis for exactly the purpose of getting us back to those hidden values so little understood by the modern man.'[1]

Viewed on the subjective plane, every symbol in the dream is a representation of something in the dreamer's psyche: a function, a quality, a tendency, being portrayed either in the guise of a real person, or by an archaic symbol. If the former, it is someone in whom that particular characteristic is prominent. There is no fixed interpretation of symbols. If it were possible for two people to dream exactly the same dream, it would still have a different meaning for each, because their associations would be dissimilar. The variety of the symbolism is unbounded, as might be expected from the vastness of the material which the unconscious has at its command. To give one instance: The attainment of individuality may be represented by such dissimilar images as the possession or finding of jewels, the sun, the king, or the queen;

[1] Jung, *Lectures* (unpublished).

SIGNIFICANCE OF DREAMS

in the case of a woman, by the birth of a child—anything which suggests the highest value. Everything depends on the associations.

In the case of dreams from the personal unconscious the symbolism comes from the life experiences of the dreamer. But not all dreams belong to that category. The connection between dreams and mythological material, between their images and the buried debris of the life of the past, whether of antiquity or of hundreds of thousands of years ago, which Jung has worked out in his collective unconscious, makes the synthetic method of dream interpretation of infinitely greater richness and fulness of meaning than a merely reductive and causal interpretation. And that these archaic, or archetypal, images occur in dreams is undeniable. The following is an instance:

The dreamer seemed to be lying on her back in bed. On her left hand in the bed she discovered an arm which was not her own. Not in the least disconcerted but very much interested, she seized the arm and examined it by touch all the way down to the fingers, two of which she put into her mouth,

THE MIND

biting them as hard as she could. The associations given were: 'The arm of the Lord;' 'the arm of the law;' and 'cannibalism.' Cannibals do not devour human flesh because they prefer it to any other, but in order that they may obtain *mana*; i.e., the strength, courage, skill, or other virtue of their enemy, which they believe they receive into themselves and assimilate by eating him. Therefore, cannibalism stood for *power*, as obviously the other two associations did also.

The dreamer had been working at too high a pressure, and the strain had left her mentally depleted. She had lost her psychic energy and needed refreshment and strength. The unconscious reacted to this conscious condition, and compensated by providing a strength-giving image, an arm, to eat. Perhaps the objection may be raised that such an interpretation is far-fetched. It may be urged, if the dreamer were weary and needed strength, surely a well-spread table of ordinary food would supply the image of refreshment. So it would if actual food had been needed. But this was not so. The dreamer's hunger was symbolic, and its satisfaction must be symbolic also. She

SIGNIFICANCE OF DREAMS

wanted a fresh supply of psychic energy and vigour—in a word, of mana. She sank in the dream to a level of the collective unconscious, where in grim earnest in the far-distant past she might have sought what she needed by eating the arm of a victim. On such a level the will is quiescent, and instinct is predominant. The archaic symbol of cannibalism was therefore necessary to represent the archaic instinct, and in itself it brought a fresh access of strength. Any collective symbol will do this. Why does the music of the national anthem or the sight of the national flag inspire a soldier with fresh courage and vigour in the hour of weariness or peril? Because they are symbols of Fatherland and of home and of all that these connote. The glory of the past, handed down through the generations, is in the collective unconscious, and, translated into terms of the present, is stronger than the individual's pain and fear, and comes rushing up to nerve and inspire him through the symbol.

The symbolism of dreams comes from all ages, historic and pre-historic. It is as though the unconscious had collected pro-

THE MIND

perties from the beginning of time, and costumes in which to array the actors of our dream life—as is indeed the case. Mithraic symbols, such as the cave or the bull; initiation ceremonies, suggesting the birth of a new attitude to life; mythological motives, such as the tree of life, the water of life, or the river of death; magical animals, gods and demons—all form part of the imagery of dreams. Sometimes an unconscious myth is worked out in a whole series of dreams. Three short examples may be given: the first of Mithraic symbolism, the second of pagan, the third is mythological.

The scene of the first dream was a Gothic cathedral in which mass was being celebrated. Suddenly, the whole side-wall of the cathedral caved in, and herds of cattle with ringing bells trooped into the church.

The setting of the second dream was also a Catholic church. But it contained a bare altar on which a naked victim lay, 'doing penance,' the dreamer thought in the dream. Here we have a pagan sacrifice in a Christian church.

The third dream was a picture of two figures. The dreamer found herself stretched

SIGNIFICANCE OF DREAMS

full length, face downwards, on the back of a cow, trying to promote a flow of milk by pressing its sides. The representation was of Hathor the Cow-goddess. The dreamer and the animal were one and the same, the unconscious suggestion being that she should seek strength and sustenance within her own nature.

The majority of dreams are of minor importance except to the dreamer, for whom they have always a meaning; but at crossroads or crises on the path of life very often arresting or even awe-inspiring dreams occur. These examples may fitly be supplemented by one of such an awe-inspiring nature. The quotation is from Jung's unpublished lectures.

This dream is ' reported by Lucius Coelius, an historian of the Second Punic War, and concerns a dream of Hannibal's before the undertaking of the war against Rome. Hannibal dreamed he was in an assembly of the gods themselves, not of their statues merely, and that Jupiter ordered him to undertake the war against Rome, and gave him as guide a youth of supernatural powers, chosen from among the divine gathering.

THE MIND

This youth told Hannibal to follow his lead, but on no account to look back as he went. However, being unable to overcome his curiosity, Hannibal did look back and saw that what was following him was a most extraordinary monster, a sort of serpent which was wiping out of existence everything they met—houses, gardens, and woods. The interpreters said that this dream meant that he should risk the war, and that the serpent stood for the destruction of Italy. Hannibal touches the divine in his dream and is given a being with superhuman powers to be his guide. This figure has the meaning of God and expresses the superhuman element in Hannibal. That guide is to lead him into great deeds, but the divine thing is also responsible for the monster that follows.

If we take the picture presented in Hannibal's dream, first the god, then the man, then the monster, we have a fair representation of the make-up of a great man.

One could say, too, that it is just that way a great man is met in the world. People are first aware of his superior power, of his mana ; then they begin to notice his human side ; and finally they realize that destruction, the

SIGNIFICANCE OF DREAMS

serpent, follows in his wake. Greatness is inevitably destructive on one side . . . To Carthage Hannibal was a Superman, but to Italy he was the destroying serpent.

The dream of Hannibal is concerned with the birth of a great deed, that is the campaign in Italy. The fact that Hannibal hesitated to risk war showed that he was not aware of the extent of his own powers, and the unconscious had to show him his greatness. Therefore, in the words of the dream, he was called to the assembly of the gods and told by Jupiter himself what lay before him. He was given a divine guide in this undertaking because the unconscious knows what it means to follow the command of a god.'

One further example of a dream may be given. In this case the unconscious voiced a warning. The dreamer who was just beginning to be analysed was staying in a London hotel. She dreamed she went up a staircase leading to her bedroom. It was like, yet unlike, the real staircase, for the steps were uncarpeted and the treads worn and ancient-looking. The door of the room faced her at the top, and she seemed to know it was a haunted room. Between the door

THE MIND

and herself were the figures of two friends. One was seated and bending forward as if ill. The other spoke and said they had been in the haunted room, but had been obliged to come out as it had made her friend feel sick and faint. The dreamer, who was in a gay, scoffing, adventurous mood, was not to be deterred and stepped lightly into the room. At that moment a physician known to her came along the corridor, and with a look of deadly seriousness, advised her ' in view of her nervous constitution ' to come out of the room. The dreamer neither saw nor heard anything to alarm her, but such was the uncanny and awesome atmosphere of the room itself that all her defiant venturesomeness evaporated and she came out.

The dream was intended as a caution that the unconscious must not be approached in a spirit of levity. The dreamer was interested intellectually, but was far from apprehending the seriousness of the venture she was making. For psychological analysis is like religion in that it involves, besides increased knowledge of oneself, a change of heart and attitude to life. The unconscious contains the Yea and the Nay—both good and evil.

SIGNIFICANCE OF DREAMS

He who undertakes to explore its depths in a serious and humble spirit reaps good he knew not of in himself ; but levity and dishonesty of spirit inevitably bring reprisals.

In concluding this short outline, a word should be said respecting Jung's attitude towards the sexual imagery so often occurring in dreams. Freud, as is well known, reduces it to repression of the sex-instinct. Jung's view is different, and more reasonable. Everything depends on the individual and on his associations. In certain cases, repression would be the correct explanation. But most frequently the images are symbolic. The urge of the creative principle is in everyone, and, in the primitive language of dreams, it is apt to be expressed by sexual symbols, and must be so understood.